BOLD KIDS

Structural Components Of Atoms

DISCOVER INTRIGUING FACTS
CHILDREN'S SCIENCE BOOK

The basic structure of atoms includes the tiny nucleus and energy levels where the electrons reside. These energy levels are sometimes referred to as rings. Neutrons have the most mass of any atom, followed by protons.

Protons are positively charged, while electrons are negatively charged and have almost no mass. They move around the nucleus in these energy levels. The most basic way to identify these different parts of an atom is through the Bohr model.

ELECTRONS

The structure of an atom is made up of the structural components, which include electrons. Electrons are atoms' primary constituent and will spend about 90% of their time in one of its orbitals.

Each orbital has its own shape and energy level, and the electrons in the s orbital can only have two electrons, so anything above 2 requires them to fill one of the other orbitals.

The atomic model was first developed in 1913 by Niels Bohr, who described the electrons as "shells" around the atomic nucleus, similar to planets orbiting the sun. Each electron has an energy level of one or more, and moves between them by either absorbing or losing energy.

The more electrons in an atom, the more positively charged it will be as a whole. The atom will then be negatively or positively charged.

Electrons are the subatomic pbooks found in an atom. They are far smaller than neutrons and protons, and their size is equivalent to eighty-three feet. They carry an electric charge, which is why they are responsible for atoms interacting with each other.

The atom has three basic components: the nucleus, protons and electrons. Each one carries a positive or negative charge. Neutrons are neutral, and have equal numbers of positive and negative charges.

The atoms contain a large percentage of empty space. The electrons add very little mass to the atom. The nucleus, on the other hand, has the greatest density.

Thus, if the electrons were completely empty, the atom would be as large as a pea! However, this does not mean that the atoms don't have a nucleus. They orbit so far away from the nucleus that they don't contribute much mass to the atom.

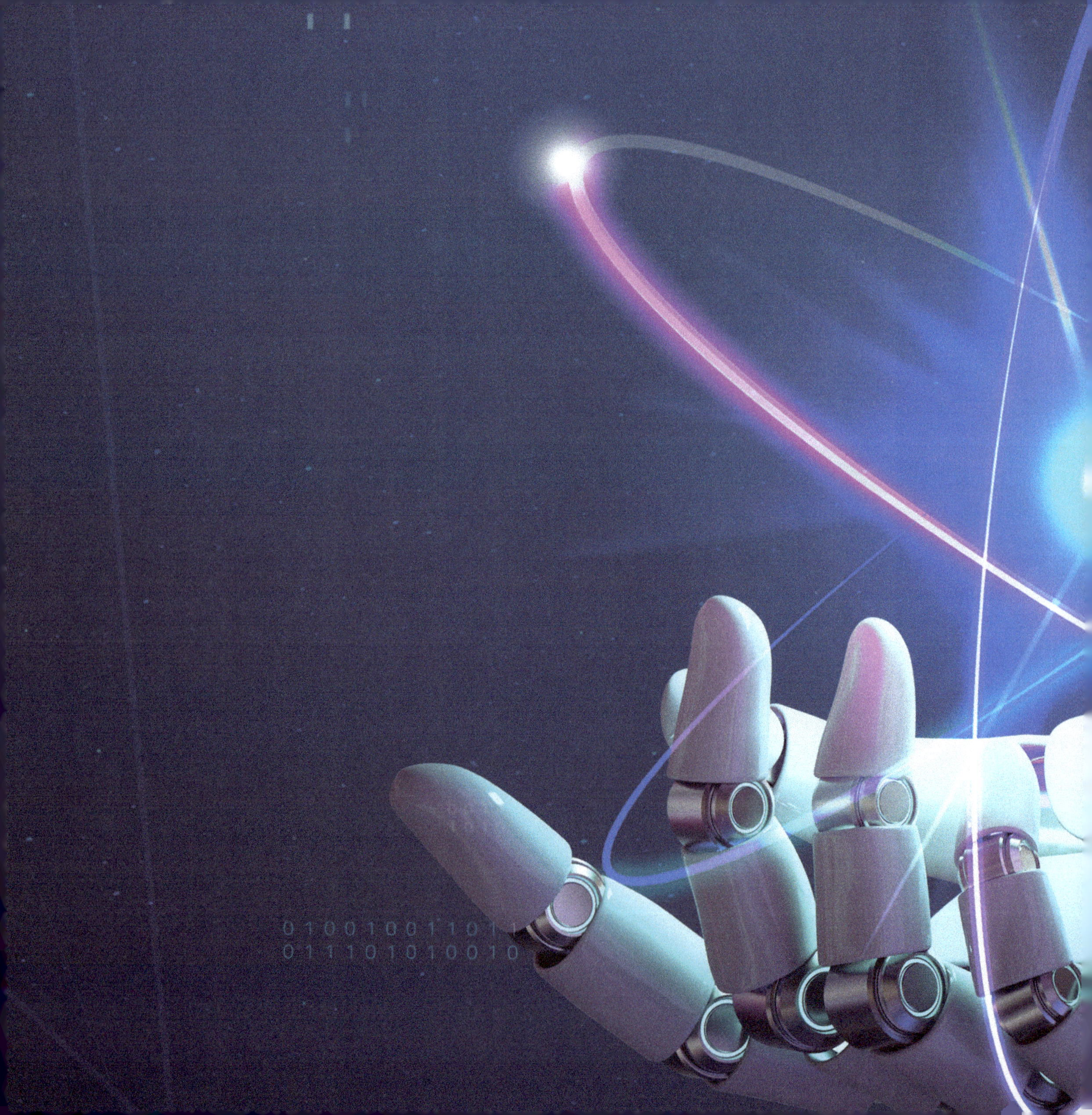
0 1 0 0 1 0 0 1 1 0 1
0 1 1 1 0 1 0 1 0 0 1 0

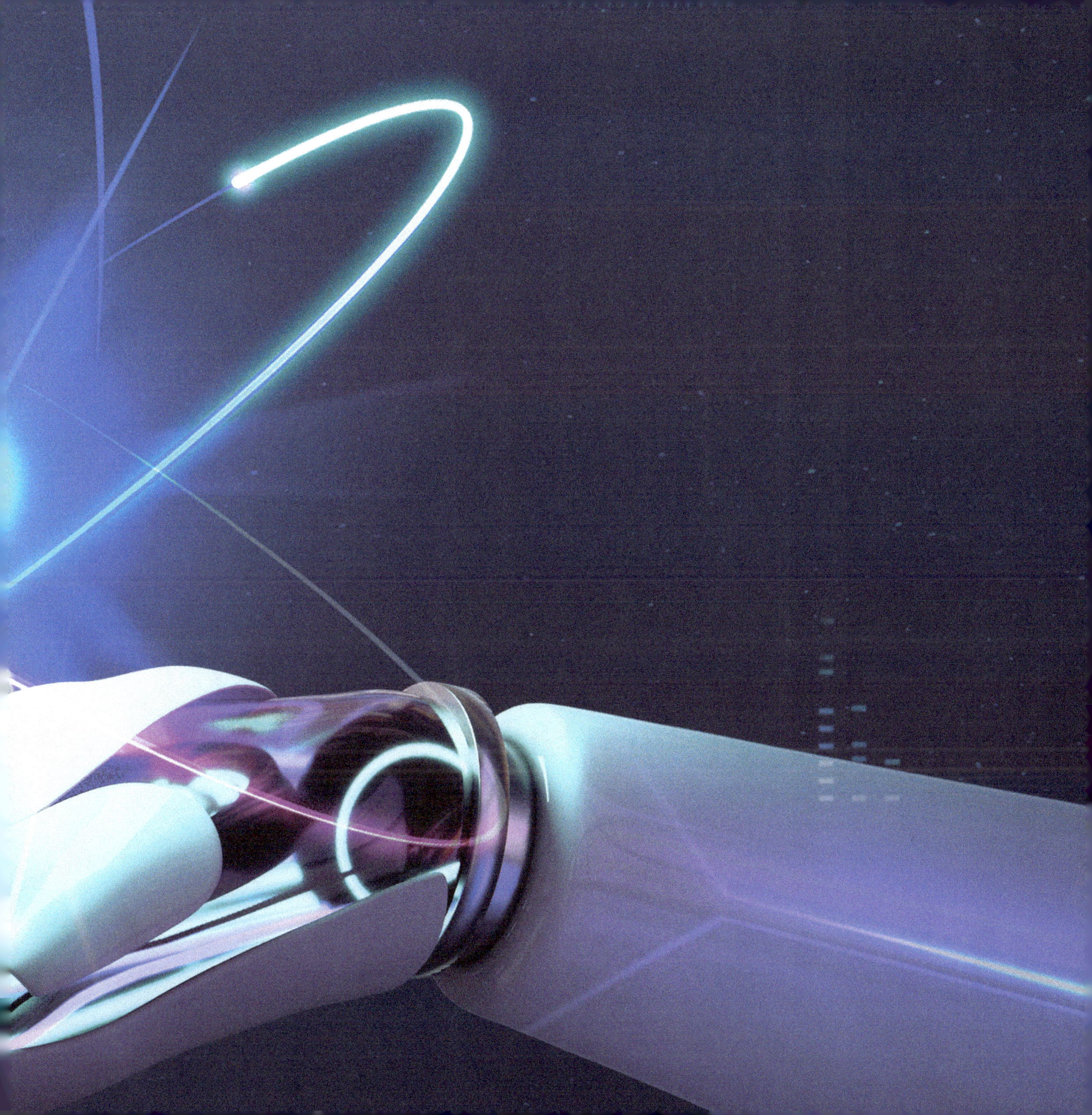

Protons and electrons have the same mass, but their mass is nearly one thousand times smaller. The mass of an atom is 1.67 x 10–24 grams, while an electron weighs around one amu. In addition to mass, electrons also contribute to the charge of an atom.

The negative charge of an electron is equivalent to the positive charge of the proton. Thus, an uncharged atom has the same number of protons as it does of electrons.

Generally, electrons are more comfortable with one atom than with another. Therefore, they are often paired in the outermost shell of an atom. This allows atoms to share electrons with other molecules.

This is how water molecules form their lattice structure. In a chemical reaction, molecules of different elements share electrons. In some cases, an atom has more than one ion, so an ion has more electrons than a cation.

Another fact about electrons is that they can deviate from their spherical symmetry. The amount of deformation depends on the size of the force and the type of electrons in the outer shell.

Some compounds with low symmetry lattices can develop large crystal-electric fields. Chalcogen and sulfur ions have been known to exhibit ellipsoidal deformations under these conditions.

PROTONS

Atoms are small, positively charged pbooks that have a central nucleus surrounded by shells of negatively charged electrons. These atoms are about the size of a human hair and contain 99.9% of their total mass in the nucleus.

In addition to protons and neutrons, atoms also contain electrons. The protons and electrons in an atom have the same charge, but opposite signs. This makes them attractive to each other.

A molecule consists of two types of atoms – a proton and a neutron. A proton contains a positive charge, while a neutron carries a negative charge. Both of these types of pbooks are found in atoms.

Electrons are tiny pbooks of matter with no known components. A molecule's atomic number and mass are determined by the mass of these pbooks.

In a chemical molecule, protons are the most abundant element. Hydrogen has one proton, while Lithium has three. Compared to protons, neutrons are slightly heavier.

Therefore, hydrogen has a higher density than Lithium. The density of hydrogen is greater than that of oxygen, while its mass density is smaller than that of oxygen. For more information, see the periodic table:

In a chemical molecule, the protons are positively charged pbooks found in an atom's nucleus. They make up the bulk of an atom and contribute more than half of its atomic mass. Their mass is also used to determine the identity of an element.

Their number and position in an atom are determined by the atomic mass. Electrons, on the other hand, orbit around the nucleus in clouds, but they do not contribute to the mass of the molecule.

As the primary subatomic pbooks, protons are a crucial part of an atom. The number of protons in an atom determines the type of atom that it is. For example, oxygen atoms contain 8 protons, while carbon atoms contain six.

Gold atoms contain 79 protons. If you change the number of protons in an atom, you change its type. This process is known as nuclear decay.

All chemical elements contain a specific number of protons. The atomic number of a substance is determined by the number of protons and electrons that are present in the nucleus. For example, carbon has six protons and six electrons.

However, the number of neutrons varies. For this reason, different elements have different atomic numbers. These are called isotopes. In chemistry, the ratio of protons to electrons determines the chemical properties of the molecule.

Neutrons and protons are the two most common atomic pbooks. They make up the nucleus, which is the basic building block of an atom. A neutral atom has equal numbers of both protons and electrons.

However, in certain cases, electrons are lost to make the atom more stable. The differences between atoms are the reason for the various characteristics of each element. The different types of isotopes are categorized according to the number of protons and electrons in them.

CPSIA information can be obtained
at www.ICGtesting.com
Printed in the USA
...V071604161222
...LV00007B/263